NAVAJO

of CANYON de CHELLY

◆◆

IN HOME GOD'S FIELDS

Rose Houk

With primary research by
Tracy J. Andrews

Southwest Parks & Monuments Association
Tucson, Arizona

Frontispiece: Navajo man carves a weaving tool while woman constructs a loom.

Title page: Early Navajo dwelling in Canyon de Chelly.

Copyright 1995 by Southwest Parks and Monuments Association, Tucson, Arizona. All rights reserved.

ISBN 1-877856-54-1
Library of Congress Number 94-69815

Editorial: Sandra Scott

Design: Christina Watkins

Typography & Production: Triad Associates

Lithography: Heritage Graphics

Photography:
Amon Carter Museum, Fort Worth, Texas. Laura Gilpin Collection. Copyright 1981—Pages 24, 30-31; 44-45; 48.
Joel Grimes—Cover, pages 27, 37.
Canyon de Chelly National Monument, National Park Service—Page 35, by T. Cronyn.
Hubbell Trading Post National Historic Site, National Park Service—Pages 53, 66.
George H.H. Huey—Pages 9, 63, 74.
Museum of New Mexico—Page 14, photo by Nicholas Brown, Neg. No. 9826; page 15, Neg. No. 44516; page 67, photo by Ben Wittick, School of American Research Collections, Neg. No. 16032.
Museum of Northern Arizona—Page 61, photo by Peter Pilles, Neg. No. 72.482.
Northern Arizona University, Cline Library, Special Collections & Archives—Page 3, Philip Johnston Collection, Neg. No. 413.194; page 22, Philip Johnston Collection, Neg. No. 413.192; page 57, Florence Barker Collection, Neg. No. 226.91.
Monty Roessel—Pages 1, 19, 23, 32, 33, 38, 41, 47, 51, 55, 60, 73, 80.
Western Archeological and Conservation Center, National Park Service, Tucson, Arizona—Page 11, photo by Charlie Steen; pages 12-13, photo by Parker Hamilton, Neg. No. 58.952; pages 58-59, photo by George Grant; page 69.
Wupatki National Monument, National Park Service—Page 56, photo by Bradley, Neg. No. W-72; page 64, photo by W.C. Bullard, Neg. No. W-1558; page 65, photo by W.C. Bullard, Neg. No. W-1556.

CONTENTS

INTRODUCTION

For nearly three centuries, the Diné, the Navajo people, have lived in Canyon de Chelly. When they arrived here in the 1700s, they found an environment especially well suited for agriculture. For three centuries, the canyon has been home, refuge, and breadbasket.

The Navajos of Canyon de Chelly were, and still are, farmers, herders, and orchardists. They grow corn, squash, beans, melons, peaches, and alfalfa, and herd sheep, goats, and cattle.

Their lives have been ruled by the land—the dictates and rhythms of its rock, sand, and water. The people of Canyon de Chelly pay close attention to every part of the land. They know what soil will grow the best corn, where water spills off the canyon walls, and where the grass grows greenest. As they work the land, they sing the songs created for them by the Holy People. As they travel through the land, they carry corn pollen, for they say "pollen is our body."

Land is used more than owned. The right to use it is based on long-standing family and clan ties. Today approximately seventy-five extended families maintain rights to use lands in Canyon de Chelly and its largest tributary, Canyon del Muerto.

Each spring, children, parents, and grandparents go into the canyons to ready their fields for planting. They place the sacred corn into the moist ground. Then, as farmers everywhere do, they await the miracle of green sprouting from the earth. They wait too for the summer rains to water their corn. They erect scarecrows in the fields and orchards to keep away the raccoons and squirrels. And early each day, after saying their prayers to the rising sun, they take their sheep to grass and water.

In autumn, they harvest the crops and save seeds for next year's planting. Whatever the bounty, they share it with their family and others. Meals of roast corn, mutton stew, and dried peaches feed their bodies and their souls.

When the harvest is in, they return to homes on the canyon rims or in the nearby town of Chinle, where travel is easier, fuelwood is available, and access to schools, services, and utilities is better. Winter is the season of storytelling and certain dances and ceremonies.

Stories are still told of the raiding Utes and the Spanish and American soldiers. A handful of determined Navajos clung to fortresses and strongholds in Canyon de Chelly even as thousands of their kin were exiled hundreds of miles away. But the people returned to the canyon, always a special place in the Navajo world, and resumed their agricultural and pastoral ways.

The Diné of Canyon de Chelly have experienced dramatic changes in their lives. Cash replaced sheep as currency. Tractors replaced digging sticks, pickup trucks replaced horses and wagons, grocery stores replaced baskets of corn. Family members go to jobs in town or in the mines, and children and grandchildren go to schools, often some distance away.

There have been moments in their history when the people of Canyon de Chelly might have been defeated forever. But strong spirits, hearts, and beliefs in how life should be lived have carried them. Ties to land, home, and sacred places are unbroken. The Diné are still here, doing what they've always done and changing as necessary. The elders are still telling the stories and singing the songs, so the young people will know.

HOME GOD'S FIELDS

In the spring, as the full moon set and the warm sun rose over Canyon de Chelly, Home God and his family went out to plant their corn. As they did so, Home God sang this song:

The holy blue corn seed I am planting.
In one night it will grow and be healthy.
In one night it grows tall,
In the garden of the Home God.

The holy white corn seed I am planting.
In one day it will grow and ripen.
In one day the corn grows tall.
In beauty it grows.

The songs of Home God and his field are a part of Navajo ceremonies, and Canyon de Chelly is a central home in the songs. These songs tell of the Navajos' long history as farmers here and their bonds to the land.

Archeological and historical information indicates the Navajos, or Diné, migrated into the Southwest from Alaska and Canada around A.D. 1525. Their new homeland, Dinétah, was centered in the canyons and mesas of northwestern New Mexico, between the four Sacred Mountains.

Originally hunters and gatherers, Navajos quickly grasped the advantages of agriculture and adopted farm crops and cultivation techniques from Puebloan people. In 1630, Spanish priest Alonso de Benavides wrote that "these Apache de Nabaju are very great farmers for this is what Navajo signifies . . . great planted fields."

Pressed by Spanish expansion, Ute raiding, and perhaps the presence of Puebloan refugees in Dinétah, Navajos began to move west and south into the Canyon de Chelly area, at the western

Canyon de Chelly from Tsegi Overlook, autumn.

edge of their territory. The exact time of their arrival in the canyons is uncertain, but it was likely after 1700. Earliest tree-ring dates taken from the wood from Navajo homes and ladders are around 1750.

As one elderly Navajo woman has told, Canyon de Chelly was settled before Canyon del Muerto, partly because del Muerto was full of wild animals and thick vines and trees, which made travel difficult and dangerous. Finally, though, men cleared away the growth and people moved there as well.

By the time the Navajo arrived in Canyon de Chelly, the stone houses the Anasazi had built in the canyon alcoves had been abandoned for nearly four hundred years. During those four centuries, others passed through the area from time to time. Villagers from the Hopi mesas and the northern Rio Grande pueblos farmed seasonally in Canyon de Chelly and sometimes used vacant Anasazi dwellings. Though the Puebloans left before the Navajos came, some may have sought refuge here again in the 1700s.

Navajo farmers in Canyon de Chelly in the early 1800s rarely enjoyed a peaceful, agricultural existence. Instead, their lives were set against a backdrop of continued raiding and retribution with Utes and Spaniards over land, livestock, and slaves. This warfare has been recorded in rock art drawn by Navajos on the walls of the canyons. Several panels show armed Spaniards on horseback, sometimes bearing lances, and one extensive panel actually depicts a battle with Ute warriors carrying shields and riding horseback among people on foot who are armed with bows and arrows.

One notable encounter between Spaniards and Navajos took place in Canyon del Muerto on a January day in 1805 when Lieutenant Antonio Narbona, commander of Spanish troops, came in search of Navajos to take into slavery. A Navajo version of the story recounts that most of their men were out on an expedition, with only old men, women, and children left behind.

The Navajos hid on a ledge high up on the sheer canyon wall, but their presence was revealed when an old woman shouted insults at Narbona and his troops as they passed by.

The Spanish troops then inched up the canyon wall, under a futile barrage of rocks and arrows thrown by the Navajos. Narbona reported that he attacked "a great number of enemy Indians [who had] entrenched themselves in an almost inaccessible spot." And "with greatest ardor and effort," by the following morning he counted among the dead ninety warriors and twenty-five women and children. Thirty-three Navajos were taken prisoner. At Massacre Cave, the site of the battle, bullet holes left by Narbona's riflemen can still be seen.

Navajo rock art depicting Spanish horsemen, Canyon del Muerto.

Lieutenant Narbona also captured 350 sheep, which he and his men ate and fed to their Navajo prisoners. Tacked on incidentally to Narbona's official report was a note that the center of Canyon de Chelly is "spacious and in it they have plenty of farmlands which are watered by a regular river that runs through the middle. . . ." With this, we have the first Spanish description of the canyon.

By the 1840s, Canyon de Chelly was known as a Navajo stronghold. Then, in 1849, Americans of European descent entered. Their presence through the next two decades left not only more eyewitness accounts of Navajo land use, but also brought about one of the darkest moments in Navajo history.

In that year, a U.S. Army reconnaissance under the command of Colonel John M. Washington explored the region. The chronicler of the expedition was Lieutenant James Simpson, who went nearly ten miles up Canyon de Chelly in September. Simpson's

Massacre
Cave is on
the narrow
ledge about
one quarter
of the way
down this
eight-
hundred-foot
cliff. From
the floor of
the canyon,
the ledge
and cave are
almost
hidden. The
climb up is
steep and
treacherous,
and the cliff
above the
ledge,
unscalable.

report and the drawings and maps in it are among the most detailed and valuable we have of that time period.

Simpson told of patches of corn, melons, and squash, and peach orchards as well. The Navajos were friendly to the troops, even bringing blanketloads of peaches to them. One of his men described Navajos living in summer "wherever the cornfields and stock are. In the winter they take to the mountains, where they can get plenty of wood."

In 1851, Colonel Edwin Vose Sumner, whose name would later be given to the infamous Fort Sumner, also reported peach orchards, wheat, corn, and beans growing in the canyons. But Sumner was not treated as kindly as Simpson had been. Ignoring warnings to stay out of the canyons, Sumner entered with artillerymen. The Navajos showered arrows on them, preventing them from climbing the walls. Frightened by the "lights of a thousand little fires" glowing on the canyon rim at night, Sumner

Christopher (Kit) Carson (left), and James H. Carleton, 1866.

and his men snuck out under darkness, Sumner whispering his commands to avoid detection.

Stories of the area's agricultural bounty continued. In 1853, Indian Agent Henry L. Dodge came with an expedition and enjoyed a feast of green corn, melons, milk, and cheese in Canyon de Chelly. When Captain John Walker made a major reconnaissance through the area six years later, Canyon del Muerto was known as Cañon del Trigo, or Wheat Canyon, for the wheat fields there.

But in 1863, as treaties between the federal government and the Indians were signed and ignored, a more serious expedition arrived, aimed at the ultimate conquest of the Navajos. The strategy was to strike at the heart of Navajo existence in Canyon

de Chelly—farms and livestock. Army Colonel Christopher Carson entered the canyon under orders from Brigadier General James H. Carleton.

Navajo captives at Issue House, Fort Sumner, 1866.

"This war," Carleton informed the Navajos, "will be pursued against you if it takes years . . . until you cease to exist or move." That move, under Carleton's plan, would be to a "spacious tribal reformatory" on the Pecos River in east-central New Mexico called Fort Sumner, or *Bosque Redondo*.

Carleton's grand experiment at Fort Sumner was intended to show the Indians a new way of life and, in his words, do away once and for all with the old ones' "latent longings for murdering and robbing." The next generations would then "become a contented people."

Apparently Carleton had not considered the possibility that the Navajos might already be content in their homes in Canyon de Chelly. But the sincerity of their resistance to the military's scorched-earth campaign was a strong clue.

For nearly six months, army troops swept through the canyons destroying Navajo livestock, cornfields, orchards, and homes as they went. In January of 1864, Kit Carson, whom the Navajos called Rope Thrower, declared the plan to destroy crops and livestock in Chinle Wash and the canyons victorious. His captives, he reported, were almost "entirely naked, and had it not been for the unusual growth of the Piñon-berry this year, they must have been without any description of food. This owing to the destruction of their grain amounting to about two Millions of Pounds by my command."

In that month, Captain Albert Pfeiffer led his men into Canyon del Muerto, and described it thus: "At some places it spreads out like a beautiful savanna, where the Corn Fields of the Savages are laid out with farmer-like taste, and supplied with acequias for irrigation."

Despite such pastoral descriptions, Pfeiffer's travels down the ice-covered stream bottom of del Muerto were anything but pleasant: His loaded mules broke through the ice every few minutes, and he faced constant challenges from Navajos attempting to defend their home from yet another military invasion. By means of wooden ladders, some Navajos took refuge high up on a large rock formation at the confluence of Black Rock Canyon with Canyon del Muerto. At this place, called Navajo Fortress, they engaged Pfeiffer in a battle that to this day is vividly retold by Navajos of Canyon de Chelly.

Pfeiffer's barrage convinced most of the people to surrender, though some successfully evaded the army by hiding in remote regions. Finally, on March 6, 1864, the Long Walk to Fort Sumner began. Initially, 2,400 Navajos, most of them on foot, started the four-hundred-mile journey. Another contingent of 3,000 Navajos set out a week later, followed by 1,200 more people in April. Hundreds died along the way.

Despite their efforts at building adobe houses and digging irrigation ditches, the Navajos never met success in their attempts

to grow corn at H*wéeldi*, their name for Fort Sumner. Four years of famine, disease, lack of fuel, and difficulties with Apaches also being held captive at the fort spelled the end of General Carleton's brave new society.

On June 1, 1868, a peace treaty was signed that established the boundaries of a 3.5-million-acre reservation in the former Navajo homeland. Included in the reservation was Canyon de Chelly and surrounding lands. Barboncito, a Navajo leader from Canyon de Chelly, looked with hope upon his people's return to their former home: "After we get back to our country it will brighten up again and the Navajos will be as happy as the land, black clouds will rise and there will be plenty of rain. Corn will grow in abundance and everything look happy."

Barboncito's prediction, though, was not immediately obvious to the Navajos as they resettled old family lands in Canyon de Chelly. Upon their return, they soon learned that during their first summer at Fort Sumner the army had continued to destroy their orchards and fields.

It was winter when the *Diné* arrived back at Canyon de Chelly, and they were unable to grow food, surviving instead on government rations of beef, flour, and coffee. Under terms of the treaty, each family head who began farming was to receive a small amount of tools and supplies in payment. During the next two decades those hoes, axes, shovels, wheelbarrows, plows, and cooking utensils, along with traditional farming methods, helped the Navajos begin their lives anew. Despite years of drought from 1868 until 1880, Canyon de Chelly was described by scholar Cosmos Mindeleff in 1883 as the agricultural center for Navajos. More than ten thousand people, he said, came for the fall harvest.

Since the days of Fort Sumner and the Long Walk, Canyon de Chelly has remained a special place to the *Diné* for many reasons. It has fed them and sheltered them and it is still the place where Home God sings his songs.

AMONG THE ROCKS

From the top of the great corn plant
the water gurgles.
I hear it.
Around the roots the water foams.
I hear it.
Around the roots of the plants it foams.
I hear it.
From their tops the water foams.

—Home God's Song

Snow falls on the Chuska Mountains. It lingers in the highest elevations through the winter, but in April the quiet thaw begins. Trickles of water gather and become streams, first flowing down steep gullies, then threading through the widening beds of Canyon de Chelly and Canyon del Muerto.

Some of the water is absorbed into the streambeds, while some seeps into the spaces between the grains of a thick underground layer of sandstone. The sandstone acts like a huge rock reservoir, storing water for future use. An underlying layer of shale prevents the water's further passage downward and keeps it close to the surface.

During spring, water flows fairly constantly in Canyons de Chelly and del Muerto. As the snowmelt from the mountains diminishes, the water flow slows. Often in summer the streams are dry unless a monsoon storm drops a few inches of rain in an afternoon.

One Navajo story says that Canyon de Chelly was formed this way: In a big lake lived a monster which roared when it was angry. One day, extremely mad, the monster plowed open the lake, letting the water rush out and make the canyon. The water flowed on toward the base of a mountain where another lake formed. The monster lived in this lake, still roaring, then moved

Navajo woman carrying water for cooking.

on to other places. People say they can still hear him roaring where he lives now, although no one has actually seen him.

Water did make these canyons, patiently cutting down through hundreds of feet of rock. Over millions of years the tapestried walls of De Chelly Sandstone have been exposed. The incising streams meandered along their courses, creating an endless rhythm of twists and turns through the canyons. Ravens must know these twists and turns by heart as they closely follow the contours on their flights.

Canyon de Chelly is really two canyons extending eastward into an uplift called the Defiance Plateau, of which the Chuska Mountains are part.

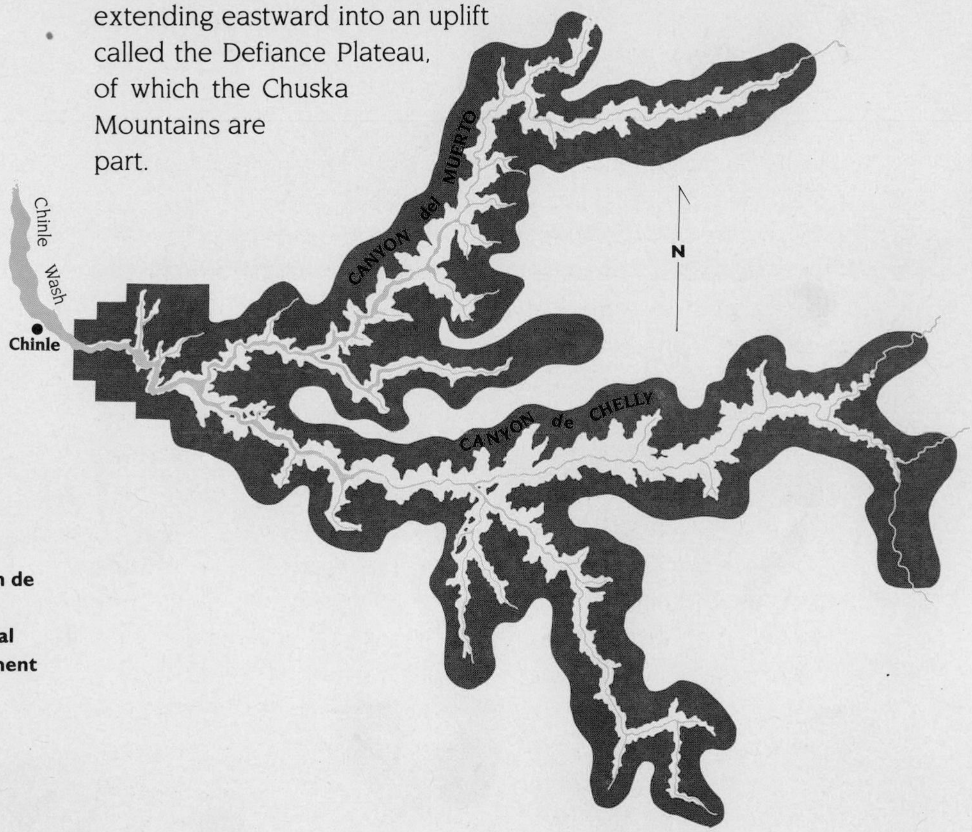

Chinle Wash

Chinle

CANYON del MUERTO

CANYON de CHELLY

N

Canyon de Chelly National Monument

Canyon de Chelly, home to Chinle Wash, is the main canyon. Its name originates from the Navajo word *tséyi'*, "rock canyon." Early Spanish maps showed it as *Chegui*, which eventually was corrupted to Chelly (pronounced SHAY). Canyon del Muerto enters from the north, meeting Chinle Wash five miles above the mouth of Canyon de Chelly at a place called Junction. The stream flows through Canyon del Muerto in Tsaile Wash. Along the length of both canyons, several lesser, but still sizable, tributary canyons—Bat, Big Flow, Black Rock, Monument, Twin Trail, and Wheatfields—contribute to the whole.

At the mouth of Canyon de Chelly near the park visitor center, the rock walls are about thirty feet high. Progressing upstream, they rise at a steady rate—200, 500, then finally, at their highest, nearly 1,200 feet high. The walls are the color of glowing copper, streaked with black desert varnish and graced with alcoves that open like giant conch shells.

Canyon de Chelly extends for about twenty-seven miles, and Canyon del Muerto about eighteen miles. The middle sections of both canyons are where the best farm lands are found. Farther up the canyons, the walls are too vertical and the slopes too rocky to provide much land for cultivation, but livestock is often grazed in these upper reaches. There are important topographic differences between the two canyons as well; del Muerto is narrower than de Chelly and meanders more. This means it has more small side canyons and large alcoves, which means more arable land.

Though breathtaking in their scenery, the canyons would not at first glance appear to be particularly good places to farm. After all, this is a high desert of rock and sand, receiving a meager nine to eleven inches of precipitation each year. And temperatures vary wildly, from above 100 degrees Fahrenheit in summer to below freezing in winter. But a unique set of topographic, geologic, and climatic factors have combined here to make Canyon de Chelly one of the best natural places in Navajoland for nonirrigated farming.

First is the proximity of the Chuska Mountains. As Chief Barboncito once observed, "In this place there is a mountain called the Sierra Chusque or mountain of agriculture from which (when it rains) the water flows in abundance creating large sand bars on which the Navajos plant their corn; it is a fine country for stock or agriculture."

Rains are important, coming as they do in the summer growing months. But as important as rain is the snow that falls in the meadows and forests high in the Chuskas. When that snow begins to melt, it delivers water to the drainages. The amount and timing of runoff in Chinle and Tsaile washes in the springtime are critical to farmers in deciding when to plant their crops. Spring runoff from the mountains comes at a most vulnerable time—when seeds and seedlings need moisture to germinate and become established. Some farmers also irrigate their fields with spring runoff before they plant.

Mud and quicksand in Chinle Wash traditionally have been a problem.

The amount and duration of water flow in the canyons are critical nowadays for another reason. In the old days, farmers often walked from the rim to the canyon bottom by way of side canyon trails, sometimes climbing up and down by means of hand and toe holds in the rock, or on wooden ladders. Now, though, most go to their fields in pickup trucks. When the water runs deep and strong to the mouth of Canyon de Chelly, access can be tricky, even with a four-wheel-drive vehicle. Tales, and actual evidence, abound of trucks mired to their door handles in mud and quicksand in the middle of Chinle Wash.

Another geologic circumstance has also contributed favorably to use of the canyons for agriculture. The De Chelly Sandstone, that makes up most of the walls of the canyons, acts as an

aquifer, or groundwater reservoir. Even more significant is the rock that underlies the De Chelly Sandstone. It is the Supai Formation, shale that is largely impermeable to groundwater flow. The existence of the Supai Formation assures a high water table, usually within three or four feet of the surface, in the Canyon de Chelly system. Canyon residents commonly dig shallow wells to reach water, both for their crops and for personal use.

The predominant De Chelly Sandstone also means that soils are mostly sandy loams and clays, which have great ability to hold moisture in critical germination time.

At this elevation—between 5,500 and 6,000 feet—the growing season averages about 145 days. Mid-May sees the last freeze in spring, and the first fall frost usually comes sometime in early October. The season is long enough to grow corn and fruit, but for well-placed individual plots it can be extended even more because the canyon walls hold heat. This advantage must be balanced against the fact that canyons are cold-air sinks at night, which has the reverse effect.

Water for household use must be collected from the wash.

From the rim overlooks, the fields are visible. They are not usually neat rectangles or squares; instead, they follow the contours of the land, tucked into an alcove or fitted onto a terrace or bench along a streambank. Fields are placed out of the streambed, sometimes against the canyon walls where they can receive water running off the cliffs, or beside the streams where water can be channeled to them. About 120 to 130 fields are in production in both canyons, a number that has stayed fairly constant since the 1950s.

Land is not actually held in private ownership in Navajo

society. Rather, land is used through a right based on family and clan relationships, a right that some say, in the traditional matrilineal society of the Navajos, was passed down through the mother's line. Since the early part of this century, all the arable land in Canyons de Chelly and del Muerto has been spoken for and field locations are stable. Because of the close relationship between kinship and land, people without relatives in the other canyon see little reason to go there, except for occasional sightseeing or picnicking.

Locations and shapes of fields make the best use of available land.

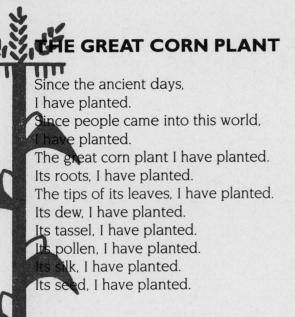

THE GREAT CORN PLANT

Since the ancient days,
I have planted.
Since people came into this world,
I have planted.
The great corn plant I have planted.
Its roots, I have planted.
The tips of its leaves, I have planted.
Its dew, I have planted.
Its tassel, I have planted.
Its pollen, I have planted.
Its silk, I have planted.
Its seed, I have planted.

—Home God's Song

Seated on a low hill of dirt that would become her corn and melon patch, Susie Brown scraped at the ground with her hoe. Her dark hair was tied up behind her neck, with two curls bobby-pinned in front. The song of a canyon wren spilled off the steep rock walls behind her.

Since early morning, Susie had been out in her field working alone, without breakfast, taking advantage of the cool shade cast by the high sandstone cliffs. It was time to rest.

The field was huge for one person to work by hand, and it was thick with weeds. Despite the daunting work spread before her, Susie expressed no interest in hiring someone to plow the field with a tractor. Her brother would be down later to help, then her sons, and after school was out for the year some of her fifty or so grandchildren would come and stay for the summer.

Susie is a Navajo woman of the Big Water Clan, a life-long resident of Canyon de Chelly. She has cultivated this piece of land each spring for many years. To get here, she said she had walked down from her winter home on the rim along the White House

Fields at the base of sandstone cliffs benefit from runoff.

Trail, a popular tourist route into the canyon. In the past, she took a closer trail, one that involved climbing wooden ladders, but this time she followed her son's advice and took the easier trail.

Susie had taken a chance and planted earlier than other canyon residents. So far, the risk seemed to have been acceptable, for her corn was three or four inches high and appeared to be thriving.

Beside her were some cantaloupe seeds in a blue cup, and in a larger plastic jug kernels of white corn floated in water. The white corn and melons went in one field, she explained, blue corn in a shady place nearby. She would also plant watermelons and tend fruit trees.

Susie said she digs a hole with her hoe, drops in a handful of kernels, covers them with soil, and waits for the rain to come. She doesn't plan to water the corn; the ground holds enough moisture for the seeds to germinate, and summer rains, if they come, will be enough for the growing plants.

Out in the field was a scarecrow dressed in jeans and an old flannel shirt. On its plastic-milk-jug head was a well-used straw hat. Susie laughed and said the scarecrow looked like her brother. She hoped it would frighten away skunks and raccoons from her corn.

Near her field stood a summer ramada, an open-air structure of wooden posts covered with tree boughs. Furnishings were sparse and utilitarian: a shelf with a few cans of food, a wood cookstove, two or three smoke-blackened pots and pans, and a small bed. Bluebird Flour sacks, reused as towels, hung from nails. Despite the thick growth of cottonwoods along the creek, wood for cooking is hard to come by in the canyon, Susie said. Piled up beside the cookstove was juniper that her sons had thrown down to her from the rim.

A weaver, Susie said she might bring her loom down this summer to use while she watches her melons grow and listens to the wind whispering in the cornstalks. Besides some hoeing, there

would be the important task of gathering corn pollen to be used in many ceremonies.

If everything went well, Susie would harvest the ripened corn in the fall and cook some in the earthen outdoor oven. First, Susie explained, she builds a large fire, then puts in whole ears of corn, covers them with dirt, and leaves the corn to steam overnight. It will be a feast for all who come.

In March or April, the fields are prepared for planting. If a field is new or hasn't been farmed for some time, brush is cut and removed and the larger trees are burned or girdled. In Canyons de Chelly and del Muerto, the spring thaw of water that froze in the fields over winter usually provides enough moisture for planting. Limited irrigation with dikes, small dams, and ditches is also practiced, mostly in Canyon del Muerto.

To know when to plant, Navajo farmers take cues from nature. Some plant from the full moon of May until the next new moon. Some say they plant when the stars of Pleiades (Dilyéhé) can no longer be seen in the sky at night. Others watch where sunlight strikes a certain place on the canyon walls. Still others wait until the leaves on the peach trees are the size of a person's thumbnail. The amount of water in the stream is now another gauge, (determining how soon trucks and tractors can get up to the fields).

Corn (naadáá') is a holy plant to the Navajos, and is the first crop planted each spring. They believe the Diné were created from an ear of corn and the skin of Changing Woman, their most important deity. Talking God says corn is the gift of life and there is no better thing. ''If you are walking along a trail and see a kernel of corn, pick it up,'' said one Navajo farmer. ''It is like a child lost and starving.''

Seeds from the healthiest, largest, and most productive ears of corn are saved from the previous year's harvest. The seeds may be gathered while the ears are still on the stalks, or after the

Cornfield and hogan flanked by towering cliffs.

ears are laid out to dry. They are consecrated in a Seed Blessing ceremony, and they may be treated with special stones, pigments, or plant concoctions to assure resistance to drought.

Navajos have several varieties of corn—white, yellow, blue, black, red, and multicolored—all well adapted to dry-farming conditions. Blue corn, favored for dumplings or cornmeal mush, is often planted apart from the other kinds.

Corn and its cultivation are of major spiritual significance to Navajos.

The cornfield is a holy place, and its layout is significant. In earlier times, a field was planted in the shape of a helix, or sun. From the center, the rows went clockwise out to the east, south, west, and north in an expanding circle. Always the right songs were sung before, during, and after planting.

Planting was usually a community effort. When a farmer was

ready to plant, he put out the word and several families came to help. When one field was done, the group moved on to another until all the work was done. More often now one farmer, perhaps with the help of spouse or children, plants the fields.

A planting stick (*gish*) was made from hard wood, often from a branch of greasewood or oak. The stick was about three feet long, sometimes curved and pointed at one end. The farmer knelt on the ground and, using the planting stick, poked a hole about a foot deep, down to moist ground. Five or ten kernels of corn were dropped in, moist earth was placed in the hole, then dry dirt put on top. A small depression was formed in the soil, and a stone slab or piece of wood was set at an angle into this "cup" to funnel water to the growing plant.

Traditionally, when the corn was ready to pick, a farmer chose four corn stalks, each with four ears. The stalks were pulled out and laid with their tips pointing to the four cardinal directions, then two more stalks were laid diagonally across these four,

representing the zenith and the nadir. The rest of the harvested corn was piled on top of these six stalks. Then the ears were pulled from the stalks and husked. When the pile was finished and the harvester had reached the original six stalks on the bottom, the ears on them were husked too, in the same order as the stalks were laid out: east, south, west, north, zenith, and nadir. Called the "main seed" or "under corn," these ears were mixed with the next year's seed to insure a good crop. Special songs accompanied and described each motion of the harvest, from the crackling sound the stalks gave as they were bent, to the sounds of the ear being pulled off the stalk and the husk being stripped off the ear.

In the past, before the advent of grocery stores, it was essential that the harvest be stored in a dry place, away from marauding rodents. Globe-shaped pits five or six feet deep were dug in the field or near the summer hogan. The bottom and sides of the pit were lined with juniper bark. Once the pit was filled with corn, shredded bark was placed over the opening, and sticks, a flat rock, and a foot of dirt added on top of that. The corn would either be placed loose in the pit or put into a goat-skin or elk-hide bag buried in it. If dried properly, corn stored in this way might keep two years.

In Canyons de Chelly and del Muerto storage pits were dug in this way, but circular walls of stone or adobe were built up around the opening to provide more capacity. In other cases, the storage cists in the prehistoric ruins were used, but this could bring on War Sickness, cured only by a special dance.

The storage pit was an important idea to the early Navajos, whose survival over the winter depended upon a well-filled, secure food cache. A Navajo chant relates that during a time of famine and starvation in the country, a person dreamed of a place where there was a bin of white corn packed in cedar bark. A boy and girl were sent to look, and they returned with a handful of corn that saved the people from starving to death. They ob-

served how the bin was built, then made their own, first underground, then above ground.

In the post–Fort Sumner days, iron tools replaced wooden
ones. A modern digging "stick" might be a metal rod from a car.
Or, if a field is small, a farmer will use a hoe to make individual
holes for the seeds. Though some older people still prefer horse-
drawn plows, which allow better control of furrow depth, tractors
are used to cultivate most fields. Because few families own a

tractor, they hire the job done by
the one or two people who do.
As the field is being plowed,
someone follows the tractor and
drops the seed into the furrows.
Despite new improvements in
technology, some Navajos believe
that planting the old way, with a
planting stick, is better. The corn,
they say, comes up faster and is
stronger.

**Navajo
woman
husking
corn, ca.
1940.**

After the seeds have germi-
nated and the corn plants have pushed up through the ground, a
farmer may thin the plants and hoe weeds two or three times
during the summer. Farmers in Canyon de Chelly rarely use
chemical fertilizers; most fields are fertilized naturally with the
manure of sheep and goats that graze in them after the harvest.

And if all goes well, water will come naturally too, from the
rumbling thunderstorms of July and August afternoons, the storms
that bring what Navajos call "male" rains. A Navajo farmer
watches carefully for signs that the precious rains may be
coming—for a ring around the sun, a tilted crescent moon, or
drops of dew where the corn leaves meet the stalk. When the
heavy rains do come, waterfalls tumble down the sheer-walled
cliffs. The farmer may channel that runoff onto his fields, or divert
water from springs or the stream, if it starts to flow.

Sometimes, though, the rains don't come. If they have not come by the end of July, Navajo farmers must hand-carry water to their plants. In the worst of times, even that effort cannot save the crop. A prolonged drought in the growing season will "burn" the corn in the fields, and harvest will be slim at best.

Besides the arrival of the magical rain, a farmer has other matters to worry about. Grasshoppers, worms, rabbits, skunks, raccoons, coyotes, crows, and jays are all potential enemies of the crops. To keep small mammals at bay, people once went out, armed with slingshots, and kept constant watch in the fields. Scarecrows are still often erected, and many are delightfully creative. One standing guard in a field in Canyon del Muerto was made of the corn plant itself, a man's coat draped over the body of the stalk, the fluffy tassels at the top forming the head.

In earlier times, less overt remedies were pursued to eliminate pests. To get rid of cutworms, one practice involved putting a worm on an ancient potsherd, performing various rituals, then leaving the worm to crawl off the sherd. If it headed away from the cornfield, this was a good sign that all the worms would leave.

Each stage of the growing season has a specific name, such as "corn has sprouted," "corn turns green," or "corn about to have a baby," and is accompanied by a special farm song. When "all are white," that is, when all the husks have turned white, the corn is mature and ready to harvest. Because of their protected location, corn is ready earlier in Canyons de Chelly and del Muerto than in other parts of the Navajo Reservation. Corn planted in mid-April is ready for harvest by mid-August to mid-September.

Though the rituals are not always followed by everyone today, one thing has stayed the same: the consumption of corn. Some corn is roasted and eaten when it is fresh. The rest is laid out to dry. The dried ears are beaten with clubs or other dried ears to loosen the kernels, which are then gathered and saved for stews and soups. Most corn is roasted, then ground into meal and

In addition to corn, a variety of crops may be planted in a family's field.

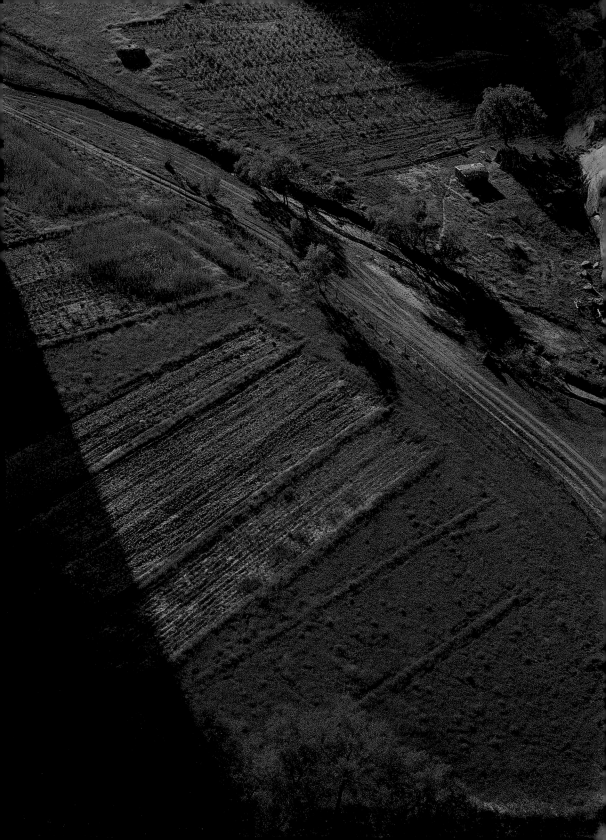

flour. The cornmeal may be sweetened and prepared into tamales, or into pancakes or a cornmeal soup by the addition of water. In the old days, grinding was done with a smooth, round handstone, or *mano*, on a concave base stone called a *metate*.

In addition to corn, Navajo farmers also plant beans, squash, watermelons, cantaloupe, tomatoes, and pumpkins. Beans are the last crop to be planted, usually in June. These legumes are put in the same rows with the corn, where they supply nitrogen. Beans are usually picked before corn. Watermelons are harvested at the first frost and are often eaten when they are still green. Almost all the foods are eaten at nearly all stages of maturity.

Gathering cornstalks to be used for cattle feed.

One elderly Navajo woman recalled that when she was a child people "would break up all the pumpkins, pack them in large sacks, then load them onto donkeys to bring them on out to the top. Doing this made it easier to bring out the harvest." Today, the harvest is usually hauled out in trucks and distributed among family members. Part of the produce may be traded for other goods; any surplus might be sold. Harvest usually takes place over several weekends when family members can come to help.

When the leaves on the cottonwoods begin to turn from deep green to waxed gold, and ice begins to line the washes, it is time to move. Autumn is the beginning of the Navajo year, when people travel out of the canyons up to their homes on the rims, where they can hunt deer, gather firewood, and harvest pinyon nuts.

Every three years or so, pinyon trees in the Southwest produce a bumper crop of big, rich, brown nuts, or *neeshch'íí'*. Once an important survival food (they kept the Navajos alive during the bleak winter of 1863-1864), pinyon nuts are still a

favorite, and their harvest means an all-day family outing in the rim forests. Pinyon seeds are eaten raw, taken back home and roasted, or ground into a butter called *'atłish*. They can also be sold and traded. Pinyon trees yield other products central to many Navajo ceremonies and medicines, and the pitch, makes an excellent waterproof seal for baskets and a glaze for pottery.

Formerly, a few families with land near the canyon mouth stayed all winter in the canyon, but now no one does. One reason is that travel along the icy streambed is difficult, but the main reason is the lack of firewood in the canyons. During the frigid winters, much wood is needed for heating homes and cooking food. Pinyon, juniper, and ponderosa are cut in the forests at higher elevations and hauled back to the rim homesites. To solve the problem of wood for the summer homes in the canyons, trucks either bring it in or, even simpler, someone stands at the rim, yells down, and throws the wood over the edge.

Winter is the time of the dances of the masked impersonators of the *Yei* gods, or Holy People, the *Yeibichei*. And it is the time when ancient games can be played. Stories and songs are planted like the corn, so that the old ways remain alive. December, the month of the big wind, once meant confinement in the hogan; and January, the month of dry snow, also was a time of restricted activity and movement. In the new moon of February, eagles laid their eggs, and in March the eaglets hatched. The annual cycle comes full circle: it is once again time to prepare the fields for planting.

MANY PEACHES

The Sun will chiefly control the trees which
are found on the surface of the earth.

—Navajo Blessingway

With binoculars, Jimmy Draper looked down at his family's home and watched his brother make coffee on an outdoor stove. An orange stop sign lay on the ground at Jimmy's feet, where the earth dropped away into Canyon del Muerto. Jimmy grew up down there, where his brother still lives. He pointed out the place where an eagle nested; he knew where bears came down from the high country; and he recalled beavers eating his family's fruit trees. Across the canyon, ruins are tucked high up on the canyon wall, near the place where Jimmy and his brother used to run races among the rocks. Near the creek stands his father's cabin. The home is called Big Falls, said Jimmy, for a waterfall that pours off the canyon walls when it rains.

From the rim Jimmy Draper can see his brother's canyon hogan.

His father, Philip Draper, started an orchard here in the upper reaches of del Muerto, irrigating with water from Tsaile Creek. Jimmy noted the ditch contouring along the hillside and recalled how his father had built a diversion dam and headgate and dug the ditch by hand. In the orchard are trees his father planted, first from apple seeds he got at the Greasewood settlement and started in tin cans. Then, said Jimmy, his father ordered seedlings from Stark Brothers Nursery in Louisiana. Philip Draper's apples often took prizes at Navajo tribal fairs.

Jimmy went out to school in Ganado, nearly forty miles away, because his father said there wasn't room for all of them on the land in the canyon. Jimmy met his wife, Ruth, at Ganado, and when they married, he brought her back to the homeplace in del Muerto. They arrived by wagon, winding through the sagebrush and juniper forest. Ruth said she believed she was coming to the "wilderness." But she and Jimmy made a life here, raising corn,

pumpkins, onions, potatoes, and fruit. At times, famine was at their doorstep and they felt lucky to get a prairie dog to eat. Even so, "we never hardly ever went to the store in those days," said Ruth. "It seemed like food was always there."

They grew all kinds of apples—Red Delicious, Romes, and Jonathans—along with cherries, apricots, and grapes. By mid-October, the trees were loaded with fruit, but the problem was getting it out to the rim along the steep, rocky trail. Everyone used to come in and get a load of ripe fruit, said Jimmy and Ruth, but even with tractors and vehicles, it was a great deal of work to haul out the produce.

Jimmy smiled as he told a story about the time he'd attached a trailer to his tractor and was driving down del Muerto. The trailer, in which Ruth was riding, came unhitched but the tractor was so noisy Jimmy didn't realize what had happened until he looked back and saw the trailer heading for the bushes with Ruth inside, laughing the whole time.

Ruth and Jimmy eventually left Big Falls for jobs in Chinle. After retiring, they took up missionary work. In summers, they have traveled to far northern Canada, where they meet Native Americans who share some of the same habits and the same words as Navajos.

As he got up to leave his spot on the rim of del Muerto, Jimmy said he wished he'd brought a newspaper for his brother, who likes to keep up with the news. Then, with a white stone, he scratched his initials on a larger rock, just to let his brother know, when he comes out the trail, whose footprints these were.

In the 1930s, a Navajo named Little Man gave an account of how fruit came to Canyon de Chelly. According to his story, a Hopi woman who had settled with the Navajos in Canyon de Chelly described her former home and the fruit trees that grew there. When Navajos went to visit the Hopi villages, they brought back peach seeds, which were first planted around White House Ruin

in Canyon de Chelly. In Canyon del Muerto, the first peaches were planted at Antelope House.

Peaches, which are not native to the Southwest, were introduced to the Hopi by the Spaniards, along with apricots, apples, pears, plums, and other fruits. But most important to the Navajos were peaches, and the Canyon de Chelly area became famous for them. Place names, such as Many Peaches Canyon off de Chelly, hint at the former abundance of this fruit. Early explorers left reports of large peach orchards in Canyon de Chelly.

During the harvest, people came in wagons from all over the reservation to trade meat, baskets, leggings, buckskins, sugar, coffee, and livestock for peaches. (A two-foot-high sack of ripe peaches was worth one sheep.) Peaches were also once traded widely for livestock, the kernels were used to polish cooking stones, the leaves to produce a yellow dye, and the fruit to induce purgative action during ceremonies.

In August of 1864 Captain John Thompson and thirty-six men marched into Canyon de Chelly to ferret out any remaining Navajos. Although Captain Thompson did not get all the Navajos to surrender, he did succeed in his other mission: destroying all the peach orchards he found. His work was systematic; he moved through the canyons, reporting his cutting tallies: 200 trees one day, 350 the next, then 100, 600, 450. One day he cut down 500 "of the best Peach trees I have ever seen in the Country, everyone of them bearing Fruit." On August 1 and 2 he managed to destroy nearly 1,800 trees. In all, Thompson personally saw to the destruction of some 4,000 fruit trees (and acres of corn and beans) in de Chelly, del Muerto, and several side canyons.

He didn't get them all, though, and in 1869, only a year after the Navajos' return from Fort Sumner, a few peaches could be found in the canyons, the only crop that survived. Twenty years later, most of the peach trees had resprouted. In the early 1880s, explorer and mapper Cosmos Mindeleff said peach trees were located in every feasible site, with a thousand trees in some

Wash meanders through Canyon de Chelly.

orchards. A special agent reported in 1891 that peach trees had grown again "from roots, stronger and better than before," but not all *Diné* have agreed with that assessment.

In the 1930s, the Indian Service sold or gave some fruit trees to canyon farmers. But a general decline in agriculture in the canyons and changes in Navajo economy and land use in this century left many of the orchards neglected and nonbearing. Erosion, a need to make a living in a cash economy, and increasing population without a corresponding increase in cultivatable land all contributed to the decline. Efforts are now underway to encourage planting of fruit trees and revitalization of orchards.

The Navajo started fruit trees from seeds rather than seedlings. They cracked open and removed the kernels from dried peach pits saved from the previous autumn. In early spring, they coated the kernels with sheep tallow, and placed a handful in a foot-deep hole. Or, a ram's horn might be placed in with the kernels. Either method helped the seeds come up quickly and made the trees strong, said orchard keepers.

Favored places for planting orchards were alluvial terraces in alcoves, mouths of side canyons, or places where runoff from the cliffs provided water. The planting site preferably had heavy soils, which hold water; alkaline soils were shunned for fruit trees. Planters dug shallow basins around young trees so they could be watered about every two weeks. Sometimes water was (and still is) carried to the seedlings from springs, streams, or hand-dug wells. The long irrigation ditch which delivered water from Tsaile Creek to the Draper orchard, and other ditches in the canyons, are not as common today as they were in the past.

When about a foot high, the most vigorous plants were transplanted to a permanent orchard, usually not far from the homestead. The trees begin to bear fruit in three or four years. Navajo orchardists never really adopted the practices of grafting or regular pruning or thinning.

Geographer Stephen Jett, who has done a great deal of

research on fruit-raising in the canyons, has noted that mammals, usually minor pests in commercial orchards, "loom large in the mind of the Navajo orchardist" because they can damage or kill trees. Throughout the time fruit was on the trees, watchers stayed in the orchards to shoot or trap pests such as foxes, squirrels, porcupines, beavers, and bears. Scarecrows or fences around individual trees now do the job. Some spraying against insects has also been undertaken in recent times. Another technique is to build fires under the trees and pile on horse manure to generate a thick, black smoke.

Early spring frosts have always been the biggest enemy of fruit trees, usually bearing delicate violet-pink blossoms by the middle of April. To protect against freezing, cedar brands from the Fire Dance were tied to trees, or burned stones from sweatbaths were placed at their base.

From early or mid-September into early October, peaches are harvested. Drought, insects, and freezes allow a respectable peach harvest only about every five years. A long time ago, fruit was gathered in willow burden baskets tied onto a person's back; more recently, a cloth tied to the tree catches the fruit as it falls.

The noncommercial, "heirloom" peaches are small, white-fleshed freestones with a sweet flavor. They are eaten either fresh, boiled, or they may be canned. More commonly they are split, pitted, and spread out to dry in the sun on flat rocks, ledges, roofs, floors of caves, and on specially prepared husking floors. One husking floor in a rock shelter was used by the same family for many years. Its 300-square-foot, smooth adobe floor was patched each harvest season.

Regular pruning or thinning of peach trees was never adopted by the Navajos.

Because the same drying places have been used repeatedly over a long period, great quantities of peach pits accumulated.

Ann Morris, wife of archeologist Earl Morris, observed in 1929 that the cliff shelter at Antelope House "had served as dumping ground for incredible masses of peach stones . . . several feet thick." As with corn, dried peaches are stored in rock or masonry pits, often beneath a cliff overhang.

Drying peaches in Canyon del Muerto.

THEIR FACES WILL BE DAWN

The Sun put down all the wild animals,
and when the sheep were placed,
this is what was said:
"Their faces will be dawn,
their eyes will be rock crystal,
their ears will be plants,
their wool will be white fog.

—Navajo Blessingway

The Blessingway, a central ceremony in Navajo religion, speaks of the placement of sheep on the surface of the earth. It expresses the Navajo belief that they have always had sheep. Wool from their sheep was used for weaving, a skill whose importance was taught to the Navajos by Spider Woman.

Herding sheep in Canyon de Chelly.

Anthropologists, tell a different story. They say that the Spanish introduced livestock—sheep, goats, and cattle—along with many animal husbandry techniques into the Southwest. Though wool came from the Spanish churro sheep, the art of weaving fine rugs and blankets, a talent for which Navajos are justly famous, was adapted from the another group, the Pueblos.

Horses too came from the Spaniards, possibly around the mid to late 1600s, and they gained great favor among the Navajos. They are used for herding livestock and for transportation, and a person's horsemanship—breaking a wild mustang or staying on a bucking bronc—is still a point of pride. In fact, galloping down the sandy bed of Canyon de Chelly on a bright October morning, the cottonwoods glowing golden against an improbably blue sky, is one of life's finer experiences.

For the Navajo people, livestock and pastoralism as a way of life and economy marked a change from total reliance on farming and hunting, a change that has been described as revolutionary.

By 1795, New Mexico Governor Fernando de la Concha

observed that the Navajos "possess much cattle and sheep, and a proportionate number of horses. In general they occupy rugged mesas of difficult access, and pasture their livestock on the borders of the Rio Puerco [of the East] and in the Cañon de Chelly. . . ." By the nineteenth century some Navajos, such as headman Narbona, had become wealthy owners of large herds, and were called *ricos*.

During the periods of warfare and raiding with the New Mexicans and United States military, most of the Navajo flocks were destroyed. When the Navajos returned from Bosque Redondo, however, the federal government encouraged them to raise livestock, and issued some 15,000 sheep and 2,000 goats to the Navajos on their new reservation. They proved so good at breeding the animals that the numbers of stock multiplied swiftly. By 1930 Navajos owned an estimated 1.3 million head of sheep and goats and from 30,000 to 75,000 horses. The reservation had grown correspondingly, mostly from land being added by executive order, from 3.5 million acres to more than 16 million acres. But by the 1930s, severe drought aggravated by overgrazing of the western range had reached a critical point in the eyes of the federal government.

In 1933 John Collier, U.S. Commissioner of Indian Affairs, ordered stock numbers on the reservation reduced by more than half. When rumors of such a program first hit, Navajos reacted with disbelief. As the program went into effect, they expressed angry opposition.

Horses were the first target. Navajo residents around Chinle at the time recall how horses were rounded up and brought to a corral at Garcia's Trading Post at the mouth of Canyon de Chelly. Sheep and goats were next, then cattle. Although the people were paid per head for their stock, in some cases the animals were shot and left to rot, a tragic, wasteful sight to Navajos.

The stock reduction program of the thirties can only be likened to the Long Walk in its traumatic effect among people

whose herds were the warp and weft of their lives. Tall John, owner of a large herd, told government inspectors: "If you take my sheep, you kill me. So kill me now. Let's fight right here and decide this thing." Many opponents of stock reduction did end up in jail and were prosecuted for their resistance.

Stock reduction also marked the beginning of range management and grazing districts on the reservation. This program mandated quantities of stock allowed per person, required grazing permits, and prohibited crossing district lines with stock. Gone were the days when herders moved their sheep many miles from the mesas to the valleys in search of grass and water. Some Navajos have said the old life ended then. Some even say many men, women, and children died of sadness for something that will never come back.

Stock reduction was forced upon the Navajos in the 1930s.

The census in 1930 recorded 356 Navajos living in Canyon de Chelly, and 4,000 sheep and goats being grazed there. And though de Chelly residents relied more on agriculture than did Navajos in other parts of the reservation, some canyon families did report heavy reductions in their herds. Although herd sizes are much smaller now, Navajos in Canyon de Chelly continue to keep sheep, goats, horses, and cattle. The bleating of wandering sheep echoes off the walls of the canyons, and the tinkle of their bells drifts up to the rim.

To Navajos, sheep and goats are much more than simply domesticated animals. They are a measure of a person's wealth, security, and family and social standing. Sheep and goats provide food, and no part of them is wasted. Mutton stew is always on the stove, ribs are grilled, the stomach and intestines made into blood sausage, even the head and tail are eaten. The fat is saved

for frybread, and goat's milk is used in cooking. Raw wool can be traded or sold directly, or it can be woven into rugs that can also be traded or sold.

But beyond the practical uses and income they bring, sheep and goats are symbolic. They are accepted as payment to a singer or medicine man for performing a ceremony. A person's skill as a sheepherder is something to be admired and emulated. And, a person returning home after an absence will often herd sheep for a few days to reestablish his position in the family.

At an early age, a child learns about herding sheep. Even at age three, a boy or girl may help get the sheep into the pens. An older child may go out with the herder and may be given a lamb, the beginning of his or her own herd.

Traditionally, Navajo sheepherding has followed a set daily pattern. Just before dawn the herd is brought out to graze, returned to the pen in midday when it is hot and the sheep refuse to eat, and taken back out to pasture in late afternoon. Each night the herd is brought back into a pen near the homestead.

A person may go out on foot or on horseback to herd sheep, with a dog or two tagging along to keep coyotes away. Herding sheep is a job that requires vigilance. For though sheep are the quintessential herd animal, never straying far alone, they must be watched constantly to assure the lead animal is not taking the herd down the wrong path. The lead sheep (actually often a goat, an animal more independent and curious than sheep) wears a bell, so the herder always knows where the herd is heading. The slowest sheep also wears a bell, so the herder knows where the flock ends.

The long hours tending the herds can lead to boredom. Young herders, for example, may be diverted by a ball game with their brothers and sisters. The price of inattention is that the sheep often end up in a box canyon where they will not move during the hot part of the day, or they may become mixed with another herd, requiring much time and effort to separate.

Sheep require a good deal of water. In the semiarid environment of the canyons, the proximity of water often determines the actual day-to-day herding pattern. To get to water and grass, temporary camps are set up away from the homestead.

Brothers play football during a break from herding livestock.

During winter, ice must be broken so the sheep can drink, and patches of snow must be cleared so they can get to the grasses. Spring, with its cold winds and fickle weather, is a challenging time for the herder. It's also lambing time, when pregnant ewes are taken out with the herd to have their young in the field. The newborn lambs must be brought back to the homestead quickly so they can be kept warm. Lambs often are bottle-fed if for some reason they cannot nurse. Sometimes rams and ewes must be kept separate to delay breeding, which must be gauged closely. If lambs are born too late in the spring they won't gain enough weight in time for market in the fall.

Sheep and goats are sheared in the spring too, sometimes goats first because their mohair often fetches a better price than sheep wool. By late spring and early summer, the sheep are counted, vaccinated, and dipped to get rid of ticks and to clean the wool.

A sheep dipping is a big community event. Several owners bring their flocks into a central place where the sheep are driven from holding pens into chutes which lead to a vat of "dip." The confused, scared animals sometimes pile up in the chute, forming chaotic bottlenecks that have to be unplugged. Everybody helps, making lots of noise to keep the herds from mixing, and poking the animals with long staffs to get them into the vat and out into the dripping pens.

In Canyon de Chelly and Canyon del Muerto, a typical annual

pattern is to take the sheep into the canyons in spring, when grama, sacaton, and needle-and-thread grasses are ripe, and where lambing can occur in a more protected place. Sheep also graze shrubs such as saltbush and sagebrush to get the salt they need in their diets. In summer, as less water is available, herds are moved to other locations within the canyons or back up to the rims. In fall, when seeps and springs begin to flow again, herds are moved back onto pasture that has had a chance to rest from grazing. Then, in winter the animals are moved to grazing lands on the rims or on the Peninsula, a high mesa area between de Chelly and del Muerto.

Spring sheep shearing, 1958.

These movements vary, depending on the size and number of a family's traditional land-use areas. If the land-use area is small, livestock may have to be grazed in a fenced field after the crops are harvested. If a family is large, wealthy, or has several recognized use areas, livestock may be moved more freely to reach pasture.

Another crop and a different kind of livestock have come into the Navajo repertoire more recently—alfalfa and cattle. Alfalfa production began in the canyons in the early 1900s, possibly encouraged by traders who supplied seed and accepted alfalfa for payment of debts. The federal government also supplied seeds in partial payment for work on projects. By 1928, alfalfa was a major crop in the Tsaile and Lukachukai creek areas, where families were attracted by farming development. A ready market for the alfalfa existed at nearby Fort Defiance.

Alfalfa has some advantages over corn—it is a perennial that

needs replanting only every three or four years. But an alfalfa field requires plowing, dragging, and levelling. Alfalfa must be harvested and hauled more frequently (requiring investment in a tractor and baling equipment), and it uses much more water than corn. Dependable irrigation is crucial for alfalfa. Seasonal flashflooding in the canyons makes keeping irrigation structures such as brush diversion dams intact a nearly futile effort. They must be repaired and rebuilt frequently, and any kind of permanent structure is mostly out of the question.

Sheeping dipping, 1923.

Early on, wealthy Navajo stockmen from the Fort Defiance area sold some cattle in Canyon de Chelly. But not until 1950 did cattle ranching begin in earnest on the Peninsula and the rim of Canyon del Muerto. With it came a demand for alfalfa for feed. Most acreage in alfalfa now is in del Muerto, and most of the families who grow alfalfa use it solely for cattle feed. If alfalfa production is good (four cuttings in a season are common), they can save on the cost of hay for winter feed. At times, too, families may sell their alfalfa crop for cash.

Cattle have one major advantage over sheep and goats—they do not require constant attention. They find their own water and don't have to be herded as closely. Cattle are pickier than sheep about what they'll eat, but they do not crop the grasses as close to the ground.

Like sheep, though, cattle are moved seasonally from canyon bottom, to the upper canyons, and onto the rims to graze. And as with sheep, these movements depend upon grass conditions, water supplies, and location of family land and permanent residence. In some instances, cattle may be left in one place all year, as for some families who have permanent residences on the

Navajos
herding
sheep in
Canyon de
Chelly.

Peninsula. Likewise, if a family's permanent residence is on a range management unit (a seeded, fenced area designated by the tribe), cattle will be left there year round. The fenced management units were established with the goal of developing small-scale, profitable ranching operations, and some families are moving in that direction.

Since their introduction by Spaniards, horses have become an integral part of Navajo life.

A decision to take up cattle ranching depends on whether a family has range management units, and whether they have enough cash to buy cattle. For many today, the decision is made because it frees their children from the constraints of sheep herding so they can go to school or take wage jobs. Cattle in the canyon area are beef, mostly white-faced Herefords. Occasionally they are butchered to eat, but more often they are seen as a good capital investment— calves bring more per pound at market than do lambs.

As in cattle operations everywhere, roundup and branding in late summer is a family or community affair. Workers build a big juniper fire, heat the branding irons red hot, and the cowboys lasso and wrestle each bawling calf to the ground. They brand the calves and castrate the young bulls. Though heifers and steers carry different brands, all the cattle have the Bar-N brand of the Navajo Nation seared into their hides.

Sheep herd going up White House Trail, 1972.

THE DAYS SINCE FORT SUMNER

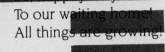

Oh, beautiful upon the earth,
All things are growing.
I hear the voice
That quickens now the earth.
So, happily may we return
To our waiting home!
All things are growing!

—The Pollen Path

From the time Navajos came to Canyon de Chelly and Canyon del Muerto, their settlement and land use have been affected by outside influences. Historically, the Navajos settled in alcoves, in major side canyons, and on talus slopes where their stone and log hogans were camouflaged from Ute and Spanish raiders. They stored food under well-hidden ledges and in alcoves, sometimes reusing the storage bins in the prehistoric pueblos.

Between 1800 and the 1860s, Navajos also settled among the pinyon-juniper forests of the canyon rims, where their buildings would be inconspicuous, in rock shelters, or on ridges, wherever they had good visibility of their surroundings. During these years, because of pursuit by United States military, they avoided benches along canyons, wide valleys, or grasslands.

Spider Rock, located at the mouth of Monument Canyon, is eight hundred feet tall.

After the return from Fort Sumner in 1868, Navajos resettled in the rim forests of Canyon de Chelly and Canyon del Muerto, perhaps for easier access to Fort Defiance and the trading posts for rations and supplies. Then, with changes in agricultural technology and without the threat of military or other intrusions, they eventually moved out into the canyon bottoms. Fields were situated to permit floodwater irrigation, and homes were placed in the open, away from the cliffs to avoid rockfalls.

Architectural styles show a continual adaptation. In some cases, prehistoric pueblos were reused by the people of Canyon

de Chelly, but with some risk. Entering the homes of the Anasazi, the "enemy ancestors," was looked upon unfavorably. More often, they constructed traditional hogans. The earliest hogans had a foundation of forked sticks, later ones had stone foundations and log roofs or were made entirely of wood. Square, masonry, log-roofed cabins also appeared, perhaps reflecting military, trading post, or Mormon influences. Often a complex overlay of architectural styles is seen at a single location, such as at Standing Cow in Canyon del Muerto.

Forked-stick hogan.

Though not always lived in today, hogans (*hooghan*, literally "place home") are still kept because certain ceremonies can be performed only in them. A hogan is one room, with a hearth in the center and a smokehole in the roof, but that single open space is divided invisibly into several smaller, symbolic spaces. Traditionally, upon entering the east-opening doorway women went to the right, or north side, of the hogan where the kitchen and loom were located. Men went to the left or south side. The back of the hogan was the seat of honor for the man or woman who was head of the family.

Building a hogan is a serious task. A proper site must be chosen and a trip made to the high country to obtain the right size juniper logs for the main poles and the ceiling beams. When the hogan is completed, it must be properly blessed.

A typical canyon farmstead today is situated with reference to farm land, stock water, pasture, and firewood. It consists of a hogan or other house where parents, children, and members of the extended family live. Around the hogan are various outbuildings, lamb pens, corrals, a summer shade or ramada, a privy, storage structures, a beehive oven, drying racks, watering troughs,

a rug loom, and piles of firewood. Today the entire homestead may be fenced to mark boundaries and to keep out livestock.

One institution—the trading post—had especially far-reaching effects on Navajo economy, land use, and settlement after the return from Fort Sumner. The first trading posts on the Navajo Reservation were set up at Fort Defiance around 1868. It wasn't long before they came to nearby Chinle and Canyon de Chelly.

As soon as they received licenses from Washington, D.C. (with good recommendations from the local Indian agents), the earliest traders set up improvised businesses in tents. Little Mexican, or Nakai Yazhie as the Navajos called him, did just that in 1882 at the mouth of Canyon de Chelly. But his was a short-lived enterprise, lasting only about a year.

Into the vacuum stepped John Lorenzo Hubbell, who had a thriving post at Ganado about thirty miles south of Chinle. Hubbell joined efforts with C.N. Cotton and in 1886 received a license to trade at Chinle. They operated out of an old stone hogan, to **Stone hogan.**

which they added three rooms of heavy, hand-hewn rock in the style of Hubbell's other posts. Trade during the first year, though, was not so prosperous. Hubbell and Cotton soon sold the post.

Some years after selling his first post, John Lorenzo Hubbell built a larger, more elaborate post on a hill at Chinle. Ahead of his time, Hubbell saw Canyon de Chelly's potential as a tourist attraction. To the trading post he added a second story with bedrooms and a dining room to accommodate visitors. But tourism did not develop as swiftly as Hubbell had hoped; only a few intrepid adventurers were willing to brave the stream crossings and sandy roads of the reservation in those days.

One of Hubbell's clerks was Leon (Cozy) McSparron, who in 1919 bought a post in Canyon de Chelly. Under McSparron's ownership, the post, which had been built in 1902 by Sam Day, Sr., became the Thunderbird Ranch (now Thunderbird Lodge). By this time, tourists were coming to Canyon de Chelly in some numbers, and McSparron accommodated them in his cabins and guest rooms. Tours into the canyon were a big attraction, first by horse-drawn wagons and later in Model T Fords. About a mile from the Thunderbird toward Chinle, on the site of the first Hubbell store, Camille Garcia also ran a trading post.

Inside, nearly all trading posts looked the same: they opened into a small area called the bullpen, surrounded on three sides by high, wooden counters. They were heated by a woodstove and lit by candles or kerosene lamps. Goods were brought to the posts by wagon, and the shelves behind the counters were stocked with flour, sugar (which Navajos called sweet salt), coffee, calico, canned fruit, candy, yarn, beads, tobacco, rope, and harness leather.

Bull pen at trading post.

Most trade was a process of barter. Sheep, wool, rugs, peaches, and pinyon nuts were brought in by the Diné and surrounding tribes. The trader paid in tokens or "scrip," which in turn was the currency he accepted for items sold in the post. A trader might also accept buttons, made of hammered silver coins, off the Navajos' clothes.

Traders and trading posts served many roles beyond simply merchant and mercantile. At a post, Navajo residents from far and wide could catch up on the latest news and gossip, get help with business affairs, or even

have the trader or his wife deal with medical emergencies. Traders, and sometimes their families, lived in quarters attached to
the post, and most of them spoke Navajo.

Sam Day's Trading Post, 1890.

    While livestock and crops could be used in trade and to pay
off winter debts to traders, eventually Hubbell, McSparron, and
others wanted Navajo rugs and silverwork more than they wanted
sheep or corn. With an eye toward commercial enterprise, they
played a large part in encouraging and shaping Navajo weaving
and jewelry making. With crafts bringing in income, and with the
availability of food and tools at trading posts, some Navajo
families could support themselves in ways other than sole depen-
dence on farming.

    Railroads arrived simultaneously with trading posts, and had
equally far-reaching impacts on the Navajos. In 1881, the tracks
of the Atlantic and Pacific Railway were completed into northern
Arizona, following the Puerco River and giving birth to the towns
of Sanders, Holbrook, Winslow, and others. The railroad drew

traders, opened outside markets for Navajo wool and crafts, brought Anglo homesteaders, and provided jobs for many Navajo men. The social and economic changes in the lives of the Navajos of Canyon de Chelly were hastened even more. Chinle grew into a community, with a post office in 1903 and Catholic mission in 1904, and soon became a regional headquarters for tribal and federal governments.

Until the 1930s, the influences of trading posts and the railroad simply grew stronger. Then, besides the drastic livestock reduction program instituted by the federal government, a number of other significant events occurred in Canyon de Chelly. Some of them, intended to encourage agriculture, have had unforeseen results.

Beginning in the 1930s (and continuing regularly into the 1960s), various federal agencies such as the Soil Conservation Service and Indian Irrigation Service carried out erosion control projects in de Chelly and del Muerto. The original plan was to build a double line of fences along streambanks, and between the fences plant various trees and grasses to form a permanent barrier against erosion. Behind that barrier, the stream would drop silt, creating fertile farmland.

The fences weren't built, but trees, tens of thousands of them, were planted to stabilize streambanks and halt outward erosion. Cottonwoods were growing along the creeks before that time, but much more sparsely than they do now. Russian olives, willows, tamarisks, and reeds were put in. Some of the trees that were planted, such as Russian olive and tamarisk, are not native to North America but they proved so prolific that canyon residents say the dense growth of trees takes up moisture and shades their fields. Offending cottonwoods are commonly burned, cut down, or girdled to kill them.

Erosion as a natural phenomenon has been known since prehistoric times in the canyons. In addition, a well-documented cycle of erosion began in canyons throughout the Southwest in

the 1880s. Both human and natural forces and activities have led
to severe lateral and vertical erosion. What this has meant to land
users in the Canyon de Chelly area is not just loss of arable land,
but also lowering of the water table. As a stream channel deep-
ens, fields that formerly could be irrigated by ditches off the

stream are now out of reach of the runoff. Fields are literally left
high and dry. As the streambed widens, fields are simply wiped
out. Once-productive fields are now marginally productive or not
productive at all without substantial investment in pumps, pipes,
and other remedies. And erosion continues—both downcutting
of the channel and sidecutting of the banks.

Along the wash, trees planted to forestall erosion are evident. Photo ca. 1954.

The federal government's presence became known in another central way in 1931, when Canyon de Chelly National
Monument was created. The National Park Service was charged
with administering 131 square miles of land in the canyons and

within one-half mile of the north and south rims. But Canyon de Chelly differed from other national monuments because the land remained with the tribe, and Navajo residents could continue to live within the monument and pursue customary land uses.

National monument designation meant more jobs for local people, but raised questions about who was responsible for what resources and how visitation should be handled to guarantee the residents' privacy. Today, the Park Service protects the prehistoric ruins and cultural aspects, while Navajos control who comes and goes in the canyons and how the land is used.

The treaty of 1868 that established the reservation also made education compulsory. The earliest reservation schools were run by the federal government or by churches. Most were boarding schools, where children were sent for the entire school year. They could return home only for holidays and during the summers.

Initially, zealous teachers and school administrators employed methods now looked upon with disfavor. Children's hair was cut, they had to wear white people's clothing, and they were punished for speaking the Navajo language. Many people resisted because the separation was painful for families, and parents feared their children would lose sight of the Navajo way of life. In 1954, a day school was established in the community of Del Muerto on the north rim of Canyon del Muerto. Many families moved there so their children could attend the school rather than be sent away to a boarding school.

World War II brought even more dramatic changes for Canyon de Chelly and the rest of the Navajo Nation. Navajo men went away to war, seeing places and experiencing events beyond their imaginings. The war created defense-related wage jobs for thousands of Navajos, but mostly in border towns and off the reservation. When the war was over, the job market dried up for many, and wage income dropped or disappeared.

After World War II, a complex series of conditions— environ-

mental changes, livestock reduction, population increase, limited size of the reservation, and a cash economy—contributed to declining reliance on traditional agriculture and herding. Statistics on livestock ownership provide one measure of these effects—in 1958, 46 percent of all reservation households had sheep and goats; by 1974 that figure had dropped to 33 percent.

A dam built in the early 1960s has also affected Navajo agriculture and land use in the canyons. Tsaile Dam, which forms Tsaile Lake at the head of Canyon del Muerto, was built by the tribal government as a flood control and recreation project. Since the dam's construction, some del Muerto residents have reported a decline in the water supply in Tsaile Creek. Jimmy Draper's brother has complained that each year there is less water for irrigating the family's orchard. Another resident said her family's move to their land in the canyon is predicated upon water releases from the dam. Before the dam was built, spring runoff down the creek was heavy but brief. Now the dam is opened in spring, and the water runs until midsummer, preventing them from reaching their home until that time. Midsummer is late to plant because the fields are too dry or because of the risk of an early autumn frost. Consequently, the woman said, the corn harvest is less than when they went in and out of the canyon by horse and donkey.

Tsaile Dam created an urgent problem in the late 1970s. Canyon residents were evacuated for several months, just at harvest time, because the dam was leaking enough to encourage fears that it might breach. Although the lake was drained and the dam reinforced, that didn't help all the canyon farmers who were ready to harvest their crops.

From the 1970s to the present, off-reservation jobs and schooling picked up once again, further disrupting the traditional extended family. For people who have continued to farm and raise livestock, technology such as trucks and tractors—along with the need to accommodate wage work—has altered both

scheduling and methods of planting. For many, farming has become a weekend event, when children and other family members can come home to help. For others, farming is no longer an annual, but a more sporadic, activity. When asked if they will be farming in a given year, many Navajos say they haven't for some years, but that their family is thinking about it again.

Again, statistics tell some of the story of what has happened to agriculture in the canyons. The total number of fields in de Chelly and del Muerto has not varied much from 1935 to 1980. But, total acreage in cultivation has declined by 28 percent—from 344 to 246 acres; cultivated acreage has declined more in Canyon de Chelly than in Canyon del Muerto. And the amount of land in de Chelly that can be irrigated without the use of capital- and labor-intensive technology has also declined to nearly nothing.

The reality today is that no family can rely totally on farming for support. In fact, even for those actively involved, farming contributes only about 10 to 20 percent of their total income.

Yet the strong agricultural heritage of Canyon de Chelly has stayed alive. Older people continue to watch the sun on the walls of the canyon. They feel the pull of the moon, and must go to their fields in the canyons, work the soil, and plant the corn. People of the younger generation are trying, despite heavy odds against them, to observe the traditions.

Lupita Litson, a young Navajo woman, speaks of her plans to build her own hogan next to her mother's. She has picked a spot beside a certain cottonwood tree, and must decide how many sides her hogan will have. She'll call on family and clan members to help select the right logs, and when her hogan is finished, she will have it blessed. With her sister, she hopes once again to farm the land in Canyon de Chelly that has been in her family since before the Long Walk.

Her memories of growing up in the canyon are of a silent place, silent until the day a big green truck roared up to their hogan and took her and her brothers and sisters away to board-

ing school in Chinle. Here they cut her long, dark hair, and she was taught to disavow her heritage.

    Yet she remained fiercely proud of her culture and her home. A bumper sticker on her car tells of her affiliation with the *Kiyaa'áanii*, or Towering House Clan. Eyes blazing, Lupita takes strong exception to a sentence she read in a book that described Canyon de Chelly as a lonely place where Navajos camp. "We don't camp here," she exclaimed, "we live here!"

    The traditional way, she explains, is to talk to the canyon, to bless the canyon before you step down into it. "You say, 'I am here and have come back to be part of you, to live with you, my sheep, my goats, my family.'"

    Near Lupita's home, the water of Canyon del Muerto joins the water of Canyon de Chelly. Her mother told her long ago that

Packing in clothes and a cot for a stay in canyon.

if she watches intently she will see where one stream actually lays on top of the other at the confluence. Though she has tried many times, Lupita has not yet seen this subtle blending, but she says she will continue to watch and concentrate even harder. For it is one of many spiritual places in this, her home.

Autumn sunset, Canyon de Chelly.

READINGS

Andrews, Tracy Joan. "Descent, Land Use and Inheritance: Navajo Land Tenure Patterns in Canyon de Chelly and Canyon del Muerto." PhD Dissertation, University of Arizona Department of Anthropology, Tucson. 1985.

——————. "Ecological and Historical Perspectives on Navajo Land Use and Settlement Patterns in Canyons de Chelly and Del Muerto." *Journal of Anthropological Research* 47(1). Spring 1991.

Bingham, Sam and Janet Bingham. *Navajo Farming.* Rock Point Community School, Rock Point, Ariz. 1979.

Bradley, Zorro. *Canyon de Chelly: The Story of its Ruins and People.* National Park Service, Washington, D.C. 1973.

Brugge, David. "Navajo Prehistory and History to 1850." *Handbook of North American Indians,* Vol. 10. Alfonso Ortiz, ed. Smithsonian Institution, Washington, D.C. 1983.

Downs, James F. *Animal Husbandry in Navajo Society and Culture.* University of California Press, Berkeley. 1964.

Evers, Larry, ed. *Between Sacred Mountains: Navajo Stories and Lessons from the Land.* Sun Tracks and University of Arizona Press, Tucson. 1982.

Fall, Patricia, James McDonald, Pamela Magers. "The Canyon Del Muerto Survey Project: Anasazi and Navajo Archeology in Northeastern Arizona." *Western Archeological Center, Publications in Anthropology,* No. 15. May 1981.

Grant, Campbell. *Canyon de Chelly: Its People and Rock Art.* University of Arizona Press, Tucson. 1978.

Hill, W.W. "Agricultural and Hunting Methods of the Navaho Indians." *Yale University Publications in Anthropology* 18. Yale University Press, New Haven. 1938.

Hooker, Kathy Eckles. Photographs by Helen Lau Running. *Time Among the Navajo: Traditional Lifeways on the Reservation.* Museum of New Mexico Press, Santa Fe. 1991.

Jett, Stephen C. "Peach Cultivation and Use Among the Canyon de Chelly Navajo." *Economic Botany* 33(3), July-Sept. 1979. The New York Botanical Garden.

——————. editor. "The Destruction of Navajo Orchards in 1864: Captain John Thompson's Report." *Arizona and the West,* Vol. 16, No. 4. Winter 1974.

Kelley, Klara B. *Navajo Land Use: An Ethnoarchaeological Study.* Academic Press, Orlando. 1986.

Thompson, Mae and Irene Silentman. "Canyon de Chelly: A Navajo View." In
Tse Yaa Kin: Houses Beneath the Rock. EXPLORATION: *Annual Bulletin of
the School of American Research*, David Grant Noble, ed. Santa Fe. 1986.

ACKNOWLEDGMENTS

My sincerest thanks to Tracy Andrews, whose fieldwork and dissertation
on Canyon de Chelly land use and agriculture provided the basic research for
this book. Her cooperation and careful review of the manuscript were
indispensable. Thanks also to Wilson Hunter of Canyon de Chelly National
Monument; Scott Travis and Tara Travis who shared the results of their
unpublished cultural landscape survey; and other monument staff who
provided assistance. Appreciation is extended to Ron Foreman and Sandra
Scott of Southwest Parks & Monuments Association.

To Lupita Litson, Susie Brown, Jimmy and Ruth Draper, and all other
native residents of the Canyon de Chelly area, I dedicate this work.

A Note on Visitation—To insure the privacy of Navajo residents, non-
Navajos may enter Canyon de Chelly and Canyon del Muerto only on
a guided Park Service or concessionaire tour. Or, a person may go with
a Navajo guide or canyon resident, with a permit obtained at the visitor
center. Access into the canyons is by foot, horseback, or vehicle. Four-
wheel-drive vehicles are required. Only one trail, to White House Ruin
in Canyon de Chelly, is open to the public without a guide.

INDEX

With the water of the dark cloud
See the blue corn grow!
With the water of the dark mist
See the white corn grow!
With this it grows.
With this it is beautiful!